This information will be made available to sensory impaired individuals upon request. Voice phone (202) 219-8615; Telecommunications Device for the Deaf (TDD) message referral phone: 1-800-326-2577.

Grain Handling

U.S. Department of Labor
Robert B. Reich, Secretary

Occupational Safety and Health Administration
Joseph A. Dear, Assistant Secretary

OSHA 3103
1996 (Revised)

Contents

Introduction

The Occupational Safety and Health Administration (OSHA) issued its Grain Handling Standard. *Title 29. Code of Federal Regulations* (CFR). Part 1910.272. in 1987 to protect workers exposed to fires and explosions. Excessive amounts of grain dust was one of the major causes of these devastating catastrophes that killed or maimed hundreds of workers.

The standard protects workers from hazards faced while walking on or underneath accumulations of grain within a grain storage facility. These hazards include engulfment and entrapment in grain and grain handling equipment, which can result in asphyxiations, crushing injuries, and amputations.

In 1996, OSHA further amended the standard[1] to protect employees whenever they enter a "flat storage structure"[2] regardless of their point of entry. "walk down" grain to make it flow within or outside of a grain storage structure or stand on grain at a depth that poses an engulfment hazard.

OSHA believes that this technical amendment will prevent from 2 to 4 additional fatalities annually and a similar number of traumatic injuries caused by mechanical devices such as augers.

Employers and employees covered by an OSHA-approved state safety and health plan should check with their state agency. which may be enforcing standards and other procedures " at least as effective as," but not always identical to. federal requirements. See list of state plans at end of this publication.

This publication serves as a guide to the standard, discusses the causes of grain dust explosions, and provides the information needed to train employees on ways to eliminate related hazards.

Scope and Application

The requirements of the standard apply to more than 250,000 workers at 24,000 grain elevators and mills that have been and continue to be exposed to fires, explosions, engulfment, and entrapment hazards. Engulfment and entrapment hazards have killed or maimed hundreds of workers.

---

[1] *Fed Reg* 61 (47):9578-9584, March 8, 1996. Part 1910.272
[2] A "flat storage structure" means a grain storage building or structure that will not empty completely by gravity, has an unrestricted ground level opening for entry, and must be entered to reclaim the residual grain by using pwered equipment or manual means.

According to the bureau of Labor Statistcs[3]. In 1993 and 1994 OSHA estimates that there have been more than 45 workers engulfed in gain and asphyxiated or crushed to death by grain augers.

Provisions of the Standard

There are several provisions employers must follow to comply with the grain handling standard. including a requirements for hot work: entering bins, silos, tanks, and other storage structures: inside bucket elevator legs: preventive maintenance. housekeeping, handling emergencies, and training.

Hot Work

A permit system is required for employees performing hot work. Hot work includes electric or gas welding, cutting , brazing, or similar flame-producing operations.

The permit is to ensure that the employer is aware of the hot work being performed—particularly, when performed by contractors—and that appropriate safety precautions have been taken prior to beginning the work.

The standard does not require a work permit if the hot work is performed in the presence of the employer or the employer's authorized representative. in an employer-authorized welding shop. or when work is conducted out of doors and away from the grain facility.

Entry into Bins, Silos. Tanks, and Other Storage Structures

Employees must be given a work permit before they enter bins, silos. or tanks unless the employer or the employer's representative is present. Such permits will help employers maintain control over employee entry into these areas.

In addition to the permit-system, employees should be thoroughly informed of the hazards associated with entry into bins, silos, tanks, and other structures. For example employees should never enter these areas from the bottom when grain or other agricultural products are hung-up or stuck to the sides. Employees should be made aware that the atmosphere in bins. silos and tanks can be oxygen deficient or toxic. Consequently, employees must be trained in the proper method of testing, the atmosphere procedures to take if the atmosphere is

---

[3] U.S. Department of Labor, Bureau of Labor Statistics, *Census of Fatal Occupational Injuries*. Washington. DC, 1993-1994.

to take if the atmosphere is found to be hazardous. The air inside the enclosure must be tested for oxygen content both before and during employee entrance, unless there is continuous natural air movement or forced-air ventilation in the space.

Provide ventilation. supplemented by the use of appropriate respirators. if necessary. If oxygen levels are less than 19.5 percent if concentrations of toxic agents present in the air either exceed ceiling limits in OSHA's health standards or will have health affects that restrict an employee's abilities to effect self-rescue or obtain assistance: or, if there is a combustible gas or vapor concentrations in excess of 10 percent of the lower flammable limit. Ventilation must be provided until the unsafe condition is eliminated and must be continued as long as there is a possibility of recurrence of the unsafe condition while the bin, silo, or tank is occupied by employees.

An employee must wear a body harness with a lifeline or use a boatswain's chair whenever entering a grain storage structure at or above the level of stored grain and the depth of stored grain poses an engulfment hazard. If the employer can demonstrate that the lifeline or boatswain's chair is not feasible or creates a greater hazard the employer must provide an alternative means of protection. Where employees work in a bin, silo, or tank, a trained and equipped observer must be present on the outside maintain communication with employees and provide help if needed.

The standard prohibits "walking down grain" to make it flow within or outside of the storage structure. or standing on moving grain. Also, all mechanical, electrical. and pneumatic equipment that presents a danger to employees inside grain storage structures must be deenergized and disconnected, locked-out and tagged, blocked-off, or otherwise stopped by other equally effective means or methods.

In addition, no employee is permitted to be in any location where an accumulation of grain on the sides of the storage structure or elsewhere could fall and engulf him or her.

Inside Bucket Elevator Legs

Inside bucket elevators are well recognized as potential ignition sources for primary explosions. To lessen these hazards, the standard requires that belts purchased after March 30, 1988, have a surface electrical resistance not exceeding 300 megohms. Bucket elevators must have an opening to the head pulley section and boot section to allow for inspection, maintenance, and cleaning; bearings must be mounted externally to the leg casing or the employer must provide vibration, temperature, or other monitoring of the conditions of the bearings if bearings are mounted inside or partially inside the leg casing.

3

Also, elevator legs must be equipped with a motion-detection device that will shut down the leg when the belt speed is reduced by 20 percent or more of the normal operating speed. A belt-alignment monitoring device with an alarm to alert employees when the belt is not tracking properly is also required: alternatively, employers must provide a means to keep the belt tracking properly.

Bearing monitors, motion detection devices, and belt-alignment devices need not be installed if the employer equips bucket elevators with a fire and explosion suppression system capable of protecting the head and boot sections of the leg, or with a pneumatic dust control system: that will keep the dust concentrations inside the leg casing 25 percent below the lower explosive limit during operation.

Preventive Maintenance

Preventive maintenance is a very important aspect of any grain industry safety and health program. It is a must for controlling fuel and ignition sources and for keeping equipment functioning properly and safely.

The OSHA standard does not require the employer to have a written preventive maintenance program but states that all mechanical and electrical equipment must be kept in proper operating condition. To do this the employer must annually inspect the mechanical and safety control equipment associated with dryers, grain stream processing equipment, dust collection equipment, including filter collectors, and bucket elevators.

This equipment must be lubricated and maintained according to the manufacturers' recommendations, or as determined necessary by prior operating records. Equipment that malfunctions or operates below designed efficiency must be promptly repaired or removed from service. Inspected or repaired equipment must how the date of inspection.

The standard also requires procedures for locking out and tagging equipment to prevent the inadvertent application of energy or motion to equipment being repaired. serviced, or adjusted. All employees who repair, service. and operate the equipment must be familiar with the employer's locking out and tagging procedures.

Housekeeping

Housekeeping is an important part of any safety and health program especially in facilities where combustible material might accumulate. The standard request the employer to develop and implement a written housekeeping program to help eliminate these dangers.

The program must include instructions for reducing dust accumulations on ledges, floors, equipment, and other exposed surfaces, and must

4

identify "priority" areas in grain elevators that are known to be potential sources of ignition. These include floor areas within 35 feet (10.9728 meters) of inside bucket elevator legs, enclosed areas containing grinding equipment. and enclosed areas containing grain dryers located inside the facility. The housekeeping program also must address the methods for removing grain spills from work areas. The use of compressed air to remove dust is permitted only when all machinery that presents a source of ignition in the area is shutdown. and all other known potential ignition sources are removed or controlled.

Because grain dust is the main source of fuel for explosions in grain handling facilities, the standard allows a maximum accumulation of more than an 1/8-inch (0.3175 centimeters) in priority housekeeping areas of grain elevators, if dust accumulations exceed the 1/8-inch (0.3175 Centimeters) action level in priority housekeeping areas designated means or methods must be initiated immediately to remove such accumulations. The standard also provides for the employer to use alternative means to the 1/8-inch (0.3175 centimeters) action level where the alternative can be demonstrated to provide equivalent protection from explosions. This may involve additional treatment of the dust and/or the area of dust accumulation, such as spraying with oil or water. In addition, the use of oil additives such as white mineral oil in the grain flow, and changes in materials handling processes can also help reduce the accumulation of dust and make the dust less explosive.

Emergency Action Plan

Employers must develop and implement a written emergency action plan. The plan does not have to be written if there are fewer than 10 employees. This plan must include a distinguishable and distinct alarm system (especially for those employees who work indoors) and evacuation procedures, and must include employee training in emergency procedures.

Employees must know where the nearest escape routes are and must be familiar with workplace maps that clearly show these emergency escape routes. In addition, at least two means of emergency escape from galleries (bin decks) are required in grain elevators.

The employer must also designate a safe area outside the facility where employees can congregate after evacuation and must implement procedures to account for all employees after emergency evacuation has been completed. It is recommended that employers seek the assistance of local fire departments to preplan for emergencies and designate a means of contacting fire and rescue agencies under emergency conditions.

Training and Education

Training employees to recognize hazards associated with their jobs is an effective method for increasing overall safe operations. Employers are required to train employees in their work tasks annually or whenever changes in job assignments expose them to new hazards. New employees are to be trained prior to starting work. Employees assigned special or infrequent tasks, such as bin entry and the handling of flammable or toxic substances, must also be trained to perform these tasks safely.

Training must include the following:

- General safety precautions associated with the grain facility as well as the recognition and prevention of hazards related to engulfment, mechanical devices, dust accumulations, and common ignition sources such as smoking.

- Specific procedures and safety practices applicable to the job tasks including, but not limited to, clearing choked legs, and performing housekeeping, hot work, preventive maintenance, and lockout/tagout. and

- Training in emergency procedures.

Other Sources of OSHA Assistance

Safety and Health Program Management Guidelines

Effective management of worker safety and health protection is a decisive factor in reducing the extent and severity of work-related injuries and illnesses and their related costs. To assist employers and employees in developing effective safety and health programs, OSHA published recommended *Safety and Health Program Management Guidelines (Federal Register 34 (I8):3908-3916, January 36,1989)*. These voluntary guidelines apply to all places of employment covered by OSHA..

The guidelines identify four general elements that are critical to the development of a successful safety and health management program:

- Management commitment and employee involvement,

- Worksite analyses,

- Hazard prevention and control, and

- Safety and health training

The guidelines recommend specific actions under each of these general elements to achieve an effective safety and health program. A single free copy of the guidelines can be obtained from the U.S. Department of Labor,

Publications, P.O. Box 37535, Washington, DC 20013-7535, by sending a self-addressed mail label with your request.

State Programs

The *Occupational Safety and Health Act of 1970* encourages states to develop and operate their own job safety and health plans. States with plans approved under section 18(b) of the Act must adopt standards and enforce requirements that. are at least as effective as federal requirements. There are currently 25 state plan states and territories: 23 covering both private and public (state and local government) employees and 2 covering public sector employees only. Plan states must adopt standards comparable (but not necessarily identical) to the federal within 6 months of a federal standard's promulgation. Until a state standard is promulgated, OSHA provides interim enforcement assistance, as appropriate, in these states. A listing of approved state plans appears at the end of this publication.

Consultation Services

Free onsite safety and health consultation services are available in all states to employers who warn help in establishing and maintaining a safe and healthful workplace. Primarily developed for smaller employers with more hazardous operations, the OSHA Consultation Service is largely funded by OSHA and is delivered by state governments employing professional safety and health consultants. The full service assistance that is offered includes an appraisal of all mechanical systems, physical work practices, occupational safety and health hazards of the workplace, and all aspects of the employer's present job safety and health program. In addition, the service offers assistance to employers in developing and implementing an effective workplace safety and health program that corrects and continuously addresses safety and health concerns.

The program is separate tom OSHA's inspection efforts. No penalties are proposed or citations issued for any safety or health problems identified by the consultant The service is confidential. The employer's name, and the firm's name, and any information about the workplace, plus any unsafe or unhealthful working conditions that the consultant uncovers will not be reported routinely to the OSHA inspection staff.

The only obligation is the employer's commitment to correct serious job safety and health hazards in a timely manner. The employer is asked to make this commitment prior to the actual visit.

For more information concerning consultation services, see the list of consultation projects at the end of this publication.

Voluntary Protection Programs (VPPs)

The Voluntary Protection Programs are designed to recognize and promote effective safety and health program management. In the VPP, management, labor, and OSHA establish cooperative relationships at workplaces that have implemented strong programs.

Sites approved for VPP's Star, Merit and Demonstration programs have met. and must continue to meet rigorous participation standards. Benefits of VPP participation include improved employee motivation to work safely, leading to better quality and productivity: lost workday case rates that generally are 60 to 80 percent below industry aver-ages; reduced workers' compensation and other injury- and illness-related costs: positive community recognition and interaction: further improvement and revitalization of already good safety and health programs; and partnership with OSHA.

Voluntary Protection Programs and onsite consultation services, when coupled with an effective enforcement program. expand worker protection to help meet the goals of the *Occupational Safety and Health Act*.

For additional information about the VPP, contact the VPP manager in your OSHA regional office listed at the end of this publication.

Training and Education

OSHA's area offices offer a variety of informational services, such as publications, audiovisual aids, technical advice, and speakers for special engagements. OSHA's Training Institute in Des Plaines, IL, provides basic and advanced courses in safety and health for federal and state compliance officers, state consultants, federal agency personnel, and private sector employers, employees, and their representatives.

Tile OSHA Training institute also has established OSHA Training Institute Education Centers to address the increased demand for its courses from the private sector and from other federal agencies. These centers include nonprofit colleges, universities, and other organizations that have been selected after a competition for participation in the program.

OSHA also provides funds to nonprofit organizations, through grants, to conduct workplace training and education in subjects where OSHA believes there is a lack of workplace training.

Grants are awarded annually and grant recipients are expected to contribute at least 20 percent of the total grant cost.

For more information on grants, courses, and education centers, contact the OSHA Training Institute, Office of Training, and Education, 1555 Times Drive. Des Plaines, IL 60018, (847) 297-4810, fax (847) 297-4874.

For further information on any OSHA program, contact your nearest OSHA area or regional office listed at the end of this publication.

Electronic Information

Labor News Bulletin Board -- OSHA news releases. recent Federal Register notices. fact sheets, and other information are available by modem by dialing (202) 219-4734. Callers should set the modem at 300, 1,200, 2,400, 9,600, or 14,400 BAUD: Parity: None: Data Bias=8: Stop Bit=1. Voice phone (202) 219-5831.

Internet -- OSHA standards, interpretations, directives, and additional information are now on the World Wide Web at http://www.osha.gov/ and http://www.osba-slc.gov/.

CD-ROM -- A wide variety of OSHA materials including standards, interpretations. directives, and more can be purchased on CD-ROM from the Government Printing Office. To order, write to Superintendent of Documents, P.O. Box 371954.Pittsburgh,PA 15250-795. Specify OSHA Regulations, Documents and Technical Information on CD-ROM, (ORDT), S/N 729-031-000005. The price is $88 per year ($ 110.00 foreign); single copy $30.00 ($37.50 foreign).

Emergencies

To report life-threatening situations, catastrophes, or fatalities call (800) 3 21-OSHA. Complaints will go immediately to the nearest OSHA area or state office for help.

For further information on any OSHA program, contact your nearest OSHA -area or regional office listed at the end of this publication.

OSHA Related Publications

Single, free copies of the following publications can be obtained from the U.S. Department of Labor, OSHA Publications. P.O. Box 37535, Washington, DC 20013-7535, (202) 219-1667 (202) 219-9266 (fax), or from the nearest OSHA regional area office listed at the end of this publication. Send a self-addressed mailing label with your request.

Consultation Services for the Employer - OSHA 3047

Control of Hazardous Energy (Lockout/Tagout) - OSHA 3120

Employer Rights and Responsibilities Following an OSHA Inspection - OSHA 3000

Employee Workplace Rights - OSHA 3021

How to Prepare for Workplace Emergencies - OSHA 3088

OSHA Inspections - OSHA 2098

Personal Protective Equipment – OSHA 3077

Respiratory Protection - OCHA 3079

The following publications are available from the Superintendent of Documents, U.S. Government Printing Office Washington, DC 20402, (202) 512-1800. Include GPO Order No. and make checks payable to Superintendent of Documents.

Construction Industry Digest - OSHA 2202
Order No. 029-016-00151-4. Cost $2.25.

Hazard Communication--A Compliance Kit - OSHA 3704
Order No. 029-016-00127-1. Cos1$18.00 (Foreign $22.50)

Hazard Communication Guidelines for Compliance - OSHA 3111
Order No.029-016-00127-I. Cost $1.00

Job Hazard Analysis - OSHA 3071
Order No.029-016-00143-3. Cost $1.00

Principal Emergency Response and Preparedness Requirements in OSHA Standards and Guidance for Safety and Health Programs - OSHA 3122
Order No. 029-O16-00136-1. Cost $2.50

Training Requirements in OSHA Standards and Training Guidelines
OSHA 2254
Order No.029-016-00137-9. Cost $4.25

States with Approved Plans

Commissioner
Alaska Department of Labor
1111 West 8th Street
Room 306
Juneau AK 99801
(907) 465-2700

Director
Industrial Commission of
    Arizona
800 W. Washington
Phoenix, AZ 85007
(602) 542-5795

Director
California Department of
    Industrial Relations
45 Fremont Street
San Francisco, CA 94105
(415) 972-8835

Commissioner
Connecticut Department of
    Labor
200 Folly Brook Boulevard
Wethersfield, CT 06109
(203) 566-5123

Director
Hawaii Department of Labor
and Industrial Relations
830 Punchbowl Street
Honolulu, HI 96813
(808) 586-8844

Commissioner
Indiana Department of Labor
State Office Building
402 West Washington Street
Room W195
Indianapolis, IN 46204
(307) 232-2378

Commissioner
Iowa Division of Labor Services
1000 E. Grand Avenue
Des Moines, IA 50319
(515) 281-3447

Secretary
Kentucky Labor Cabinet
1049 U.S. Highway, 127 South
Frankfort, KY 40601
(502) 564-3070

Commissioner
Maryland Division of Labor
    and Industry
Department of Labor Licensing
    and Regulation
501 St. Paul Place, 2nd Floor
Baltimore, MD 21202-2272
(410) 333-4179

Director
Michigan Department of Labor
Victor Office Center
201 N. Washington Square
P.O. Box 30015
Lansing, MI 48933
(517) 373-9600

Commissioner
Minnesota Department of Labor
    and industry
443 Lafayette Road
St. Paul, MN 55155
(612) 296-2342

Director
Nevada Division of Industrial
    Relations
400 West King Street
Carson City, NV 97502
(702) 687-3032

Secretary
New Mexico Environmental
  Department
1190 St. Francis Drive
P.O. Box 26110
Santa Fe, NM 87502
(505) 827-7850

Commissioner
New York Department of Labor
W. Averell Harriman State
  Office
Building – 12, Room 500
Albany, NY 12240
 (518) 457-2741

Commissioner
North Carolina Department of
  Labor
319 Chapanoke Road
Raleigh, NC 27603
(919) 662-4585

Administrator
Department of Consumer &
  Business Services,
Labor and Industries Building
  Room 430
Salem, OR 97310
(503) 378-3272

Secretary
Puerto Rico Department
  of Labor
and Human Resources
Prudencio Rivera Martinez.
  Building
505 Munoz Rivera A-venue
Hato Rey, PR 00918
(809) 754-2119

Commissioner
South Carolina Department
  of Labor
3600 Forest Drive
P.O. Box 11329
Columbia, SC 29211-1329
(803) 734-9594

Commissioner
Tennessee Department of Labor
Attention: Robert Taylor
710 James Robertson Parkway
Nashville, TN 37243-0659
(615) 741-2582

Commissioner
Industrial Commission of Utah
160 East 300 South, 3rd Floor
P.O. Box 146600
Salt Lake City, UT 84114-6600
(801) 530-6898

Commissioner
Vermont Department of Labor
  and Industry
National Life Building –
  Drawer 20
120 State Street
Montpelier, VT 05620
(802) 828-2788

Commissioner
Virgin Islands Department of Labor
  and Industry
Powers- Taylor Building
13 South 13th Street
Richmond, VA 23219
 (804) 786-2377

Commissioner

Virgin Islands Department
    of Labor
2131 Hospital Street, Box 890
Christiansted
St. Croix, VI 00820—1666
(809) 773-1994

Director

Washington Department
    of Labor and industries
P.O. Box 44000
Olympia, WA 98504-4000
(360) 902-4200

Administrator

Worker's Safety and Compensa-
    ation Divison (WSC)
Wyoming Department
    of Employment
Herschler Building, 2nd Floor
    East
122 West 25th Street
Cheyenne, WY 82002
(307) 777-7786

OSHA Consultation Project Directory

State	Telephone
Alabama	(205) 348-3033
Alaska	(907) 269-4939
Arizona	(602) 542-5795
Arkansas	(501) 682-4522
California	(415) 703-4441
Colorado	(303) 491-6151
Connecticut	(203) 566-4550
Delaware	(302) 577-3908
District of Columbia	(202) 576-6339
Florida	(904) 488-3044
Georgia	(404) 894-8274
Guam	(671) 647-4202
Hawaii	(808) 586-9116
Ida ho	(208) 385-3283
Illinois	(312) 814-2337
Indiana	(317) 232-2688
Iowa	(515) 281-5352
Kansas	(913) 296-4386
Kentucky	(502) 564-6895
Louisiana	(504) 342-9601
Maine	(207) 624-6460
Maryland	(410) 333-4218
Massachusetts	(617) 969-7177
Michigan	(517) 332-8250 (H)
	(517) 322-1809 (S)
Minnesota	(612) 297-2393
Mississippi	(601) 987-3981
Missouri	(314) 751-3403
Montana	(406) 444-6418
Nebraska	(402) 471-4717
Nevada	(702) 486-5016
New Hampshire	(603) 271-2024
New Jersey	(609) 292-3923
New Mexico	(505) 827-2877
New York	(518) 457- 2481
North Carolina	(919) 733-2360
North Dakota	(701) 221-5188
Ohio	(614) 644-2246
Oklahoma	(405) 528-1500

Oregon	(503) 378-3272
Pennsylvania	(412) 357-2396
Puerto Rico	(809) 754-2171
Rhode Island	(401) 277-2438
South Carolina	(803) 734-9599
South Dakota	(605) 688-4101
Tennessee	(615) 741-7036
Texas	(512) 440-3834
Utah	(801) 530-6868
Vermont	(802) 828-2765
Virginia	(804) 786-8707
Virgin Islands	(809) 772-1315
Washington	(206) 956-4249
West Virginia	(304) 558-7890
Wisconsin	(608) 266-8579(H)
	(414) 521-5063(S)
Wyoming	(307) 777-7786

(H)-Health
(S)- Safety

OSHA Area Offices

Area	Telephone
Albany, NY	(518) 464-6742
Albuquerque, N M	(505) 766-3411
Allentown, PA	(215) 776-0592
Anchorage, AK	(907) 271-5152
Appleton, WI	(414) 734-4521
Augusta, ME	(207) 622-8417
Austin, TX	(512) 482-5783
Avenel, NJ	(908) 750-3270
Baltimore, MD	(410) 962-2840
Baton Rouge, LA	(504) 389-0474
Bayside, NY	(718) 279-9060
Bellevue, WA	(206) 553-7520
Billings, MT	(406) 657-6649
Birmingham, AL	(205) 731-1534
Bismarck, ND	(701) 250-4521
Boise, ID	(208) 334-1867
Bowmansville, NY	(716) 684-3891
Braintree, MA	(617) 565-6924
Bridgeport, CT	(203) 579-5579
Calumet City, IT	(708) 841-3800
Carson City, NV	(702) 885-6063
Charleston, WV	(304) 347-5937
Cincinnati, OH	(513) 841-4132
Cleveland, OH	(216) 522-3818
Columbia, SC	(803) 765-5904
Columbus, OH	(614) 469-5582
Concord, NH	(603) 225-1629
Corpus Christi, TX	(512) 884-2694
Dallas, TX	(214) 320-2 400
Denver, CO	(303) 844-5285
Des Plaines IT	(708) 803-4800
Des Moines, I A	(515) 284-4794
Englewood, CO	(303) 843-4500
Erie, PA	(814) 833-5758
Fort Lauderdale, FL	(305) 424-0242
Fort Worth, TX	(817) 885-7025
Frankfort, KY	(502) 227-7024
Harrisburg, PA	(717) 782-3902

16

Hartford, CT ....(203) 240-3152
Hasbrouck Heights, NJ ....(201) 288-1700
Honolulu, HI ....(808) 541-2685
Houston, TX ....(713) 286-0583
Houston; TX ....(713) 591-2438
Indianapolis, IN ....(317) 226-7290
Jackson, MS ....(601) 965-4606
Jacksonville, FL ....(904) 232-2895
Kansas City, MO ....(816) 426-2756
Lansing, MI ....(517) 377-1892
Little Rock, AR ....(501) 324-6291
Lubbock, TX ....(806) 743-7681
Madison, WI ....(608) 264-5388
Marlton, NJ ....(609) 757-5181
Methuen, MA ....(617) 565-8110
Milwaukee, WI ....(414) 297-3315
Minneapolis, MN ....(612) 348-1994
Mobile, AL ....(205) 441-6131
Nashville, TN ....(615) 781-5423
New York, NY ....(212) 264-9840
Norfolk, VA ....(804) 441-3820
North Aurora, IL ....(708) 896-8700
Oklahoma City, OK ....(405) 231-5351
Omaha, NE ....(402) 221-3182
Parsippany, NJ ....(201) 263-1003
Peoria, IL ....(309) 671-7033
Philadelphia, PA ....(215) 597-4955
Phoenix, AZ...(602) 640-2007
Pittsburgh, PA ....(412) 644-2903
Portland, OR ....(503) 326-2251
Providence, RI ....(401) 528-4669
Raleigh, NC ....(919) 856-4770
Salt Lake City, UT ....(801) 524-5080
San Francisco, CA ....(415) 744-7120
Savannah, GA ....(912) 652-4393
Smyrna, GA ....(404) 984-8700
Springfield, MA..(413) 785-0123
St. Louis, MO ....(314) 425-4249
Syracuse, NY ....(315) 451-0808
Tampa, FL ....(813) 626-1177
Tarrytown, NY ....(914) 682-6151
Toledo, OH ....(419) 259-7542
Tucker, GA ....(404) 493-6644
Westbury, NY ....(516) 334-3344
Wichita, KS ....(316) 269-6644
Wilkes-Barre, PA ....(717) 826-6538

U.S. Department of Labor
Occupational Safety and Health Administration
Regional Offices

Region I
(CT,* MA, ME, NH, RI, VT*)
133 Portland Street
1st Floor
Boston, MA 02114
Telephone: (617) 565-7164

Region II
(NJ, NY, * PR,* VI*)
201Varick Street
Room 670
New York, 10014
Telephone: (212) 337-2378

Region III
(DC, DE,MD,* PA, VA,* WV)
Gateway Building, Suite 2100
3535 AM Street
Philadelphia, PA 19104
Telephone:(215) 596-1201

Region IV
(AL, FL, GA, KY,*MS, NC,
SC,* TN*)
1375 Peachtree Street, N.E.
Suite 587
Atlanta, GA 30367
Telephone: (404) 347-3573

Region V
(IL, IN,* MI,* OH, WI)
230 South Dearborn Street
Room 3244
Chicago, IL 60604
Telephone: (312) 353-2220

Region VI
(AR, ILA, NM,*OK, TX)
525 Griffin Street
Room 602
Dallas, TX 75202
Telephone: (214) 767-4731

Region VII
(IA,* KS, MO, NE)
City Center Square
110 Main Street, Suite 8 00
Kansas City, MO 64105
Telephone: (816)426-5861

Region VIII
(CO, MT,ND,SD,UT,* WY*)
Federal Building, Room 1576
1999 Broadway
Denver, CO 8002-5716
Telephone: (303) 391-5858

Region IX
American Samoa, AZ,* CA,*
Guam, HI,*NV,*Trust Territories of the Pacific)
71 Stevenson Street, Room 420
San Francisco, CA 94105
Atlanta, GA 30367
Telephone: (415) 744-6670

Region X
(AK, * ID, OR,* WA*)
1111 Third Avenue
Suite 715
Seattle, WA 98101-3212
Telephone: (206) 553-5930

* These states and territories operate their own OSHA-approved job safety and health programs (Connecticut and New York plans cover public employees only). States with approved programs must have a standard that is identical to, or at least as effective, as the federal standard.